LET'S GO BOURBON!

Tony Katz and Fingers Malloy

Hosts of the nationally syndicated
Eat! Drink! Smoke! radio program

CONTENTS

ACKNOWLEDGMENTS

Many thanks to Sarah Smith and Jackie Bodnar.

And with deep appreciation to Corey Johnston and the staff at Blend Bar Cigar in Indianapolis - Richard, Brian, Josh, Cesar, Nick, Akbar and Jojo.

Today's rain is tomorrow's whisky.
- Scottish Proverb

WHAT MAKES BOURBON, BOURBON?

Bourbon is the American drink. Not only through legend and history, but by law. A formal resolution defining what bourbon is, and how it must be made, was first introduced by Rep. John C. Watts of Kentucky on January 24,1963. In less than a year and a half, the resolution passed the U.S. House of Representatives and a concurrent Senate resolution passed both chambers of Congress, declaring bourbon a, "distinctive product of the United States ... unlike other types of alcoholic beverages, whether foreign or domestic."[1]

But what is it that makes bourbon, bourbon? The rules of bourbon are very simple, and cannot be broken. Take the adage to heart: ***All Bourbons Are Whiskeys, But Not All Whiskeys Are Bourbons.***

First, let's take a look at the spelling. In the United States, we spell whiskey as "whiskey." That is a uniquely American spelling of the word, and it is used on bourbon, rye, and blended products from the United States. For Scotch, or

Irish, Canadian, and Japanese products, the customary spelling is "whisky."

According to the Code of Federal Regulations, bourbon is made using specific guidelines.[3] Anything that deviates from these guidelines will change the designation of the juice inside. It can still be delicious, it can still be whiskey, but it is not bourbon.

For example, let's look at Jack Daniel's Tennessee Whiskey. It is not bourbon, but it is whiskey. Why? From the Jack Daniel's website:

> Jack Daniel's is dripped slowly - drop-by-drop - through ten feet of firmly packed charcoal (made from hard sugar maple) before going into new charred oak barrels for maturing. This special process gives Jack Daniel's Tennessee Whiskey its rare smoothness. It's this extra step - charcoal mellowing – that makes Jack Daniel's a Tennessee Whiskey.[4]

It's a special process, indeed. But by doing so, it is no longer bourbon. The rules for bourbon are as follows, in no particular order. Memorize them as you see fit. Or not, it's your life.

THE RULES OF BOURBON!

- Bourbon can only be made in the United States.
- The mash bill (the mix of grains fermented to make alcohol) must contain 51% corn, along with rye, wheat, or malted barley.
- When distilled, it cannot be higher than 160 proof (80% alcohol by volume).
- It must be aged in first-use, charred oak barrels. Charred means the barrel is burned inside before the juice is added. The amount of time for this "char" is at the discretion of the distillery. Note, these barrels are one and done. After first use, they cannot be used for bourbon again. But their usefulness is not done; you will see a lot of former bourbon barrels being repurposed in the creation of Scotch and Irish whisky.
- When placed into the barrel, it can not be higher than 125 proof (62.5% alcohol by volume). The only way to bring down the proof is to add water. Nothing else can be added if it is going to be called bourbon.
- It must be bottled at a minimum of 80 proof (40% alcohol by volume).

The definition of "straight bourbon" is also written into law, and refers to how long the juice is kept in the barrel. In order to be called straight bourbon, it must be aged in the barrel for at least two years.

In some cases, distillers will put an age statement on their product. In other cases, they won't. A distiller advertising a 7 year-old bourbon is promising that no drop of bourbon in that specific bottle has aged less than seven years in the barrel.

Another distiller might be mixing younger bourbons together to create a specific taste profile, and might not list any age statement on that blended bourbon. This is referred to as "NAS," or No Age Statement.

DO NOT THINK POORLY OF THIS BOURBON! You'd be missing out on something potentially great, and flavors that can help you grow your palate.

Then there is the concept of Bottled In Bond, dating back to the legal standards set by the Bottled-In-Bond Act of 1897. (6) The purpose of the designation was to protect the consumer. Before Prohibition, there was a lot of counterfeit whiskey. Actually, calling it counterfeit does not express enough contempt for those bastards who produced the evil swill. In many cases, it was poison. Sometimes, it was as simple as coloring or flavoring that was added. Other times, gasoline was the special ingredient.

The bottled-in-bond designation is best summed up by the American Bourbon Association:

> Bourbon classified as Bottled In Bond must have been made during a single distilled season at one distillery, aged in a federally bonded warehouse for a period of at least four years and bottled at 100 proof as originally defined in the Bottled-in-Bond Act of 1897. Only American whiskeys can carry the label of "Bottled in Bond," and any such bourbon label must identify the distillery from which it was distilled and bottled.[6]

There's so much more to learn about bourbon. But that's not the purpose of this book. This is just to get you started, and to give you the basics about the drink you love so much.

THE COMPLETE TEXT OF THE LAW

Bourbon is bourbon because Congress declared it so in 1964. While bourbon can be made anywhere in the United States (not just Kentucky) it must follow these rules. Any deviation from what is prescribed below might yield a great tasting whiskey, but it is not bourbon.

Tony Says: I'm not gonna get on a rant here about government, but you have to understand how serious these people were about setting rules and regulations. First, taxes on spirits were a great source of revenue for the government. And, as we all know, government loves collecting taxes.

Second, there is a real question here of whether these regulations saved the industry (or, maybe more to the point, helped in its creation.) We weren't joking about duplicitous characters who - trying to make a quick buck - hurt or killed people in pushing swill as bourbon or whiskey. It was ugly.

While I naturally tend to the ideas of less

government, the history here is worth thinking about.

Oh, and check out the penalties for not following the rules. Those fines were pretty steep for back in the day.

* * *

HR CONCURRENT RESOLUTION 57
88th Congress of the United States of America Introduced January 24th, 1963

Whereas it has been the commercial policy of the United States to recognize marks of origin applicable to alcoholic beverages imported into the United States; and

Whereas such commercial policy has been implemented by the promulgation of appropriate regulations which, among other things, establish standards of identity for such imported alcoholic beverages; and

Whereas among the standards of identity which have been estab- lished are those for "Scotch whisky" as a distinctive product of Scotland, manufactured in Scotland in compliance with the laws of Great Britain regulating the manufacture of Scotch whisky for consumption in Great Britain and for "Canadian whisky" as a dis- tinctive product of Canada manufactured in Canada in compliance with the laws of the Dominion of Canada regulating the manufacture of whisky for consumption in Canada and for "cognac" as grape brandy distilled in the Cognac region of France, which is entitled to be so designated by the laws and regulations of the French Government; and

Whereas "Bourbon whiskey" is a distinctive product of the United States and is unlike other types of alcoholic beverages, whether foreign or domestic;

Whereas to be entitled to the designation "Bourbon whiskey" the product must conform to the highest standards and must be manu- factured in accordance with the laws and regulations of the United States which prescribe a standard of identity for "Bourbon whiskey"; and

Whereas Bourbon whiskey has achieved recognition and acceptance throughout the world as a distinctive product of the United States: Now, therefore, be it

Resolved by the Senate {the House of Representatives concurring), That it is the sense of Congress that the recognition of Bourbon whiskey as a distinctive product of the United States be brought to the attention of the appropriate agencies of the United States Government toward the end that such agencies will take appropriate action to prohibit the importation into the United States of whisky designated as "Bourbon whiskey".

Agreed to May 4, 1964.

* * *

THE CODE OF FEDERAL REGULATIONS, 27 CFR § 5.22 - The standards of identity

(b) *Class 2; whisky.* "Whisky" is an alcoholic distillate from a fermented mash of grain produced at less than 190° proof in such manner that the distillate possesses the taste, aroma, and characteristics generally attributed to whisky, stored in oak containers (except that corn whisky need not be so stored), and bottled at not less than 80° proof, and also includes mixtures of such distillates for which no specific standards of identity are prescribed.

(1)

(i) "Bourbon whisky", "rye whisky", "wheat whisky", "malt whisky", or "rye malt whisky" is whisky produced at not exceeding 160° proof from a fermented mash of not less than 51 percent corn, rye, wheat, malted barley, or malted rye grain, respectively, and stored at not more than 125° proof in charred new oak containers; and also includes mixtures of such whiskies of the same type.

(ii) "Corn whisky" is whisky produced at not exceeding 160° proof from a fermented mash of not less than 80 percent corn grain, and if stored in oak containers stored at not more than 125° proof in used or uncharred new oak containers and not subjected in any manner to treatment with charred wood; and also includes mixtures of such whisky.

(iii) Whiskies conforming to the standards prescribed in paragraphs (b)(1)(i) and (ii) of this section, which have been stored in the type of oak containers prescribed, for a period of 2 years or more may optionally be further designated as

"straight"; for example, "straight bourbon whisky", "straight corn whisky", and whisky conforming to the standards pre- scribed in paragraph (b)(1)(i) of this section, except that it was produced from a fermented mash of less than 51 percent of any one type of grain, and stored for a period of 2 years or more in charred new oak containers may optionally be designated merely as "straight whisky". No other whiskies may be designated

"straight". "Straight whisky" includes mixtures of straight whiskies of the same type produced in the same State.

(2) "Whisky distilled from bourbon (rye, wheat, malt, or rye malt) mash" is whisky produced in the United States at not exceeding 160° proof from a fermented mash of not less than 51 percent corn, rye, wheat, malted barley, or malted rye grain, respectively, and stored in used oak containers; and also includes mixtures of such whiskies of the same type. Whisky conforming to the standard of identity for corn whisky must be designated corn whisky.

(3) "Light whisky" is whisky produced in the United States at more than 160° proof, on or after January 26, 1968, and stored in used or uncharred new oak containers; and also includes mixtures of such whiskies. If "light whisky" is mixed with less than 20 percent of straight whisky on a proof gallon basis, the mixture shall be designated "blended light whisky" (light whisky - a blend).

(4) "Blended whisky" (whisky - a blend) is a

mixture which contains straight whisky or a blend of straight whiskies at not less than 20 percent on a proof gallon basis, excluding alcohol derived from added harmless coloring, flavoring or blending materials, and, separately, or in combination, whisky or neutral spirits. A blended whisky containing not less than 51 percent on a proof gallon basis of one of the types of straight whisky shall be further designated by that specific type of straight whisky; for example, "blended rye whisky" (rye whisky - a blend).

(5)

(i) "A blend of straight whiskies" (blended straight whiskies) is a mixture of straight whiskies which does not conform to the standard of identify for "straight whisky." Products so designated may contain harmless coloring, flavoring, or blending materials as set forth in 27 CFR 5.23(a).

(ii) "A blend of straight whiskies" (blended straight whiskies) consisting entirely of one of the types of straight whisky, and not conforming to the standard for straight whisky, shall be further designated by that specific type of straight whisky; for example, "a blend of straight rye whiskies" (blended straight rye whiskies). "A blend of straight whiskies" consisting entirely of one of the types of straight whisky shall include straight whisky of the same type which was produced in the same State or by the same proprietor within the same State, provided that such whisky contains harmless coloring, flavoring, or blending materials as stated in 27 CFR 5.23(a).

(iii) The harmless coloring, flavoring, or blending materials allowed under this section shall not include neutral spirits or alcohol in their original state. Neutral spirits or alcohol may only appear in a "blend of straight whiskies" or in a "blend of straight whiskies consisting entirely of one of the types of straight whisky" as a vehicle for recognized flavoring of blending material.

(6) "Spirit whisky" is a mixture of neutral spirits and not less than 5 percent on a proof gallon basis of whisky, or straight whisky, or straight whisky and whisky, if the straight whisky component is less than 20 percent on a proof gallon basis.

(7) "Scotch whisky" is whisky which is a distinctive product of Scotland, manufactured in Scotland in compliance with the laws of the United Kingdom regulating the manufacture of

Scotch whisky for consumption in the United Kingdom: ***Provided,*** That if such product is a mixture of whiskies, such mixture is

"blended Scotch whisky" (Scotch whisky - a blend).

(8) "Irish whisky" is whisky which is a distinctive product of Ireland, manufactured either in the Republic of Ireland or in Northern Ireland, in compliance with their laws regulating the

manufacture of Irish whisky for home consumption: ***Provided,*** That if such product is a mixture of whiskies, such mixture is

"blended Irish whisky" (Irish whisky - a blend).

(9) "Canadian whisky" is whisky which is a distinctive product of Canada, manufactured in Canada in compliance with the laws of Canada regulating the manufacture of Canadian whisky for consumption in Canada: ***Provided,*** That if such product is a

mixture of whiskies, such mixture is "blended Canadian whisky" (Canadian whisky - a blend).

* * *

THE BOTTLED-IN-BOND ACT
54th Congress of the United States of America

CHAP. 379 — An Act to allow the bottling of distilled spirits in bond.

Internal revenue. Bottling of distilled spirits in bond.

Be it enacted by the Senate and House of Representatives of the United States of America in Congress assembled, That whenever any distilled spirits deposited in the warehouse of a distillery having a surveyed daily capacity of not less than twenty bushels of grain, which capacity or not less than twenty bushels thereof is commonly used by the distiller, have been duly entered for withdrawal upon payment of tax, or for export in bond, and have been gauged and the required marks, brands, and tax-paid stamps or export stamps, as the case may be, have been affixed to the package or packages containing the same, the distiller or owner of said distilled spirits, if he has declared his purpose so to do in the entry for withdrawal, which entry for bottling purposes may be made by the owner as well as the distiller, may remove such spirits to a separate portion of said warehouse which shall be set apart and used exclusively for that purpose, and there, under the supervision of a United States storekeeper, or storekeeper and gauger, in charge of such warehouse, may immediately draw off such spirits, bottle pack, and case the same:

Provisos. Mingling of same spirits.

Provided, That for convenience in such process any number of packages of spirits of the same kind, differing only in proof, but produced at the same distillery by the same distiller, may be mingled together in a cistern provided for that purpose, but nothing herein shall authorize or permit any mingling of different products, or of the same products of different distilling seasons, or the addition or the subtraction of any substance or material or the application of any method or process to alter or change in any way the original condition or character of the product except as herein authorized;

Use of bottling room restricted.

nor shall there be at the same time in the bottling room of any bonded warehouse any spirits entered for withdrawal upon payment of the tax and any spirits entered for export:

Bottling fruit brandy.

Provided also, That under such regulations and limitations as the Commissioner of Internal Revenue, with the approval of the Secretary of the Treasury, may prescribe, the provisions of this Act may be made to apply to the bottling and casing of fruit brandy in special bonded warehouses.

Bottle stamps.

Every bottle when filled shall have affixed thereto and passing over the mouth of the same such suitable adhesive engraved strip stamp as may be prescribed, as hereinafter provided, and shall be packed into cases to contain six bottles or multiples thereof, and in the aggregate not less than two nor more than five gallons in each case, which shall be immediately removed from the distillery premises.

Stamps on cases.

Each of such cases shall have affixed thereto a stamp denoting the number of gallons therein contained, such stamp to be affixed to the case before its removal from the warehouse, and such stamps shall have a cash value of ten cents each, and shall be charged at that rate to the collectors to whom issued, and shall be paid for at that rate by the distiller or owner using the same.

Brands on cases.

And there shall be plainly burned on the side of each case, to be known as the Government side, the proof of the spirits, the registered distillery number, the State and district in which the distillery is located, the real name of the actual bona fide distiller, the year and distilling season, whether spring or fall, of original inspection or entry into bond, and the date of bottling, and the same wording shall be placed upon the adhesive engraved strip stamp over the mouth of the bottle. It being understood that the spring season shall include the months from January to July, and the fall season the months from July to January.

Trademarks.

And no trade-marks shall be put upon any bottle unless the

real name of the actual bona fide distiller shall also be placed conspicuously on said bottle.

Regulations.

SEC. 2. That the Commissioner of Internal Revenue, with the approval of the Secretary of the Treasury, may, by regulations, prescribe the mode of separating and securing the additional warehouse, or portion of the warehouse hereinbefore required to be set apart, the manner in which the business of bottling spirits in bond shall be carried on, the notices, bonds, and returns to be given and accounts and records to be kept by the persons conducting such business, the mode and time of inspection of such spirits, the accounts and records to be kept and returns made by the Government officers, and all such other matters and things, as in his discretion, he may deem *requisite for a secure and orderly supervision of said business; and he may also, with the approval of the Secretary of the Treasury, prescribe and issue the stamps required.*

Filtering, reducing, etc. permitted.

The distiller may, in the presence of the United States storekeeper or storekeeper and gauger, remove by straining through cloth, felt, or other like material any charcoal, sediment, or other like substance found therein, and may whenever necessary reduce such spirits as are withdrawn for bottling purposes by the addition of pure water only to one hundred per centum proof for spirits for domestic use, or to not less than eighty per centum proof for spirits for export purposes, under such rules and regulations as may be prescribed by the Commissioner of Internal Revenue with the approval of the Secretary of the Treasury;

Regauging.

and no spirits shall be withdrawn for bottling under this Act until after the period shall have expired within which a distiller may request a regauge of distilled spirits as provided in section fifty of the Act of August twenty-eighth, eighteen hundred and ninety-four.

Inspection, etc., of spirits bottled for export.

SEC. 3. That all distilled spirits intended for export under the provisions of this Act shall be inspected, bottled, cased, weighed, marked, labeled, stamped, or sealed in such manner and at such time as the Commissioner of Internal Revenue may prescribe; and the said Commissioner, with the approval of the Secretary of the Treasury, may provide such regulations for the transportation, entry, reinspection, and lading of such spirits for export as may from time to time be deemed necessary; and all provisions of existing law relating to the exportation of distilled spirits in bond, so far as applicable, and all penalties therein imposed, are hereby extended and made applicable to distilled spirits bottled for export under the provisions of this Act,

No drawbacks.

but no drawbacks shall be allowed or paid upon any spirits bottled under this Act.

Tax to be paid on deficiency.

SEC. 4. That where, upon inspection at the bonded warehouse in which the spirits are bottled as aforesaid, the quantity so bottled and cased for export is less than the quantity actually contained in the distiller's original casks or packages at the time of withdrawal for that purpose the tax on the loss or deficiency so ascertained shall be paid before the removal of the spirits from such warehouse, and the tax so paid shall be receipted and accounted for by the collector in such manner as the Commissioner of Internal Revenue may prescribe.

Tax to be collected if export cases are opened, changed, etc.

SEC. 5. That where, upon reinspection at the port of entry, any case if export cases are containing or purporting to contain distilled spirits for export is found opened, changed, etc. to have been opened or tampered with, or where any mark, brand, stamp, label, or seal placed thereon or upon any bottle contained therein has been removed, changed, or willfully defaced, or where upon such reinspection any loss or discrepancy is found to exist as to the contents of any case so entered for export, the tax on the spirits contained in each such case at the time of its removal from warehouse shall be collected and paid.

Punishment for reusing stamps, bottles, regulations.

SEC. 6. That any person who shall reuse any stamp provided under this Act after the same shall have been once affixed to a bottle as provided herein, or who shall reuse a bottle for the purpose of containing distilled spirits which has once been filled and stamped under the provisions of this Act without removing and destroying the stamp so previously affixed to such bottle, or who shall, contrary to the provisions of this Act or of the regulations issued thereunder remove or cause to be removed from any bonded warehouse any distilled spirits inspected or bottled under the provisions of this Act, or who shall bottle or case any such spirits in violation of this Act or of any regulation issued thereunder, or who shall, during the transportation and before the exportation of any such spirits, open or cause to be opened any case or bottle containing such spirits, or who shall willfully remove, change, or deface any stamp, brand, label, or seal affixed to any such case or to any bottle contained therein, shall for each such offense be fined not less than one hundred nor more than one thousand dollars, and be imprisoned not more than two years, in the discretion of the court, and such spirits shall be forfeited to the United States.

Punishment for counterfeiting stamps, etc.

SEC. 7. That every person who, with intent to defraud, falsely makes, forges, alters, or counterfeits any stamp made or used under any provision of this Act, or who uses, sells, or has in his possession any such forged, altered, or counterfeited stamp, or any plate or die used or which may be used in the manufacture thereof, or who shall make, use, sell, or have in his possession any paper in imitation of the paper used in the manufacture of any stamp required by this Act, shall on conviction be punished by a fine not exceeding one thousand dollars and by imprisonment at hard labor not exceeding five years.

No *exemption from State, etc., laws.*

SEC. 8. That nothing in this Act shall be construed to exempt spirits bottled under the provisions of this Act from the operation of chapter seven hundred and twenty-eight of the public laws of the Fifty-first Congress, approved August eighth, eighteen hundred and ninety.

Approved March 3, 1897.

3

THIS IS NOT A BOOK FROM EXPERTS

Maybe now is a good time to let you in on a secret....

WE ARE NOT EXPERTS ON BOURBON!
Not even close. We are guys who enjoy trying bourbon. Those who dedicate themselves to distilling — who understand the detail of the grain and the nature of their copper pot, who get outrageous satisfaction from playing with a mash bill, who revel in the heat of the rickhouse — those are special people, indeed.

Us? We're two guys from Indianapolis who enjoyed a cigar and a bourbon, and wanted to learn more.

* * *

I'm Tony

When I started the "Eat! Drink! Smoke!" podcast, I was looking for a way out of politics. I wasn't trying to escape my radio career, mind you. I love hosting two daily shows out of Indianapolis, IN, both three hours each, on 93.1 FM WIBC. My morning show has been #1 in the ratings (or close to it) for over six years. My midday program airs statewide and on stations in Atlanta, GA (WSB), Tulsa, OK (KRMG), and St. Louis, MO (Newstalk STL) I spend time on TV, and I've entertained live audiences across the country.

Political and cultural talk radio is something I really enjoy doing. But we've all seen how insane politics has become — people can't even talk to each other anymore!

Unless, of course, you're in a cigar lounge.

Cable news would have you believe political rage is everywhere, but I've never seen it in a cigar lounge. Where I smoke cigars and drink bourbon, people are laughing. They're talking to each other, not at each other. They come from all walks of life: men, women, Black, White, Hispanic, Asian, Christian, Jewish, agnostic, atheist, wealthy, and working class.

Funny thing is, none of these differences matter in the lounge. It's about relaxing and enjoying the company of good, respectful, interesting people. I've had more conversations about raising kids then I have about politics. Real life is happening over a bourbon, and it doesn't resemble cable news at all.

I was immediately drawn to this culture, where people weren't obsessed with judging others and being judged. Where instead they were trying new things, listening, learning, and sharing thoughtful opinions. I wanted to be where real life was. Sure, I've heard mentions of rising gas prices, computer chip short- ages, and politics in a cigar lounge. But these topics are fleeting; they never define the experience. They are small pieces of something much greater and far more valuable.

This cigar lounge lifestyle has helped to ground me. Outside of my family and my synagogue, nothing has been more instrumental in giving my soul a place to engage.

Corny, possibly. But absolutely a fact of my life.

It was in this scene that I learned bourbon is art. And like all art, it is open to interpretation.

Let's imagine some experts have decided that "Bourbon A" is the best bourbon in the world. They have very refined palates and have conducted tremendous amounts of research. They have studied bourbon for thousands of hours. Their expertise should be respected.

But you? You think "Bourbon A" is, to quote Rodney Dangerfield in Caddyshack, low-grade dog food.

So who is right? That's the thing — you both may be right. Perhaps with more hours of study under your belt, and more exposure to bourbons and ryes and whiskeys of all kinds, you might develop an appreciation for "Bourbon A." Or maybe nothing would change, and you will still consider "Bourbon A" to be an evil thought up by North Korean scientists.

That, in a nutshell, is what I thought was lacking in the conversations about bourbon and cigars.

So, I started a podcast. I wanted to talk about bourbon in a way that gave my thoughts on it, but did not try to define it. Why? Because I am not an expert!

That was June, 2018. And over those first two years we made changes, made mistakes, and found our voice. In July of 2020, I got a phone call from a radio consultant I know:

"Hey, Tony. Is your podcast syndicated on radio?"

"Ummm. No. But it could be!"

A couple of phone calls and five days later, we signed a syndication deal and launched the show nationally. Today, the show airs on stations across the country.

"Eat! Drink! Smoke!" is not trying to tell you what to drink. We don't have a ratings system. We don't award points. We try bourbon ... and rye ... and rum ... and tequila. We share our experience and we encourage our listeners to responsibly give it a try and share their experiences, too. And, like it happens in our favorite lounges, we talk about what's happening in real life.

Our attitude is probably much like your own: You don't need to be an expert to enjoy great things, and you don't need to be lectured on the things you enjoy.

That's "Eat! Drink! Smoke!" And that is the guiding principle of this book.

* * *

I'm Fingers

Born on the south side of Saginaw, Michigan, I've seen some things, man!

I am the co-host, producer and Happy Hour anchorman of "Eat! Drink! Smoke!" I'm also a Detroit Lions fan, I love my 1972 Harley Electra Glide, and I am a hoot at parties.

I've been involved in podcasting and radio since 2009, and I host a weekend show on 92.7 FM WAAM in Ann Arbor, Michigan. The name of the show is "The Snark Factor." That's where I talk politics and pop culture with my co-host, Sarah Smith — but as you can probably guess by the show title, we don't take things too seriously.

Tony and I have known each other for over a decade. When he asked me to join his cigar, food, and bourbon podcast, I jumped at the chance. Talking about cigars and bourbon among friends is a great escape from the craziness of today's world. Now it's a syndicated show, and the best gig in radio.

Tony is the cigar guy on the show. Me? I like booze. Specifically, whiskey. When I was younger, I cared more about quantity over quality.

I drank ... a lot. College was fun.

As I got a little older and a little wiser, I started to value quality over quantity. However, quality doesn't have to mean expensive. As we talk about on the show, you don't have to spend over $100 to buy a great bourbon. Some of the best juice we have reviewed costs less than $35 a bottle.

That has been my focus on "Eat! Drink! Smoke!" I'm always looking for a good bourbon at a price that won't blow my entertainment budget.

Is the bourbon that we are reviewing in my liquor cabinet at its price point?

Yes, or no. That's the rating.

We are fans of bourbon. You're a fan of bourbon. We thought we would share with you what we've learned. That's why we wrote this book.

4

WHAT WORDS MEAN

Here is a quick and easy resource for all those whiskey and bourbon terms that get bandied about everywhere.

* * *

ABV. Alcohol By Volume. The amount of alcohol content in a beverage.

Age Statement. An explanation of how old the youngest whiskey in the bottle is. Anything less than four years old requires an age statement. If it's a blend, the age statement shows the youngest whiskey in that specific blend. Very often, whiskey aged above four years will show NAS, or No Age Statement. This allows the distillery to make blends based on taste profile, and to use other whiskeys when needed, based on production. Of course, if a bourbon is bottled-in-bond or single barrel, then there is no blend, and the age presented is the age of all the bourbon in the bottle.

Angel's Share. The amount of bourbon that evaporates while it is in the barrel.

Bottled-In-Bond. A designation created by the government to discourage counterfeiters. It refers only to whiskey produced in the same distilling season, by the same distiller, at the same distillery. It must spend four years in the barrel, and can only be bottled at 100 proof (50% ABV).

Char. The actual fire used to heat or burn the interior of an oak barrel to make it legal for creating bourbon. Sometimes referred to as "toasting."

Chill Filtration. A process of reducing the temperature of whiskey, and then passing it through filters to eliminate cloudi- ness which comes from fatty acids that bind together at lower temps. This binding, or "floccing," takes place in lower proof whiskeys, usually under 46% ABV. There is no right or wrong here. Some distillers proudly say their bourbon is not filtered, while others see the process as benefiting their bourbon vision.

Cooperage. A place that makes barrels to be used for aging bourbon. A "cooper" is the person who makes and repairs the barrels.

Distillation. The separation of components of a liquid through repeated boiling and condensation.

Dram. A unit of liquid equal to 1/8 fluid ounce. In our parlance, with a nod to its Scottish roots, it refers to a small serving of whiskey. (Fun fact: a dram is also the name of the official currency of Armenia, which is pretty cool.)

Ethanol. A byproduct of fermentation that comes from the breakdown of sugars.

Finger. A unit of liquid equal to about 1 fluid ounce. In our parlance, it refers to an old school way of ordering whiskey.

Fingers Malloy. Co-host of "Eat! Drink! Smoke!" Ask for a "Fingers Malloy" of bourbon, and you're gonna hurt yourself.

He is 6 feet, 3 inches tall ... without the mohawk!

Finish. The predominant taste left in your mouth (on your palate) after enjoying a particular drink, bourbon or whiskey.

Juice. What we, and many others, call bourbon. Or whiskey. Or whisky. Or whatever it is we are drinking.

Mash Bill. The mix of grains used to make bourbon.

Nose. The smell or aroma of a particular drink, bourbon or whiskey.

Palate. Your sense of taste.

Proof. The amount of alcohol content in a beverage. Considered to be twice the ABV.

Rickhouse. A structure holding the bourbon barrels while they age. They can be made of anything — wood, brick, stone, or metal — and are usually no higher than seven stories. Since they are rarely climate controlled, rickhouses can substantially change the flavor of the bourbon in the barrel, depending on where the barrel is placed.

Single Barrel. Whiskey that comes from one, single barrel.

Small Batch. This is very technical, so follow along carefully. Small batch means, well, nothing. It doesn't exist in any legal definition or rule about whiskey or bourbon. It's more of a term of art to denote a relatively small group of barrels that are mixed together to create a desired flavor profile.

Sour Mash. A process of distilling that uses portions of older mash leftovers to start the process of a new mash bill. Think of it in the same way that sourdough bread has a starter dough.

Still. An apparatus that allows for the distilling of liquids by heating and cooling the contents to condense the vapors.

Straight. A reference to bourbon that has aged for at least two years in the barrel.

Sweet Mash. A process of distilling that does not use old mash leftovers. Sweet mash is nowhere near as popular as sour mash. Yet.

FIVE DRINKS YOU HAVE TO KNOW HOW TO MAKE BY HEART

While many people think it heresy to add anything to their bourbon or whiskey, great mixologists have crafted magnificent works over the years.

These drinks aren't an abomination. Rather, they are great creations. They have history and subtle complexities ... and they are fantastic. True, knowing how to make these cocktails will give you a chance to show off in front of your friends (or that particular person you're looking to impress). But making these, tasting these, and sharing these recipes will also help to grow your own personal appreciation of the hobby we all enjoy.

* * *

Old Fashioned

Ingredients

3 oz. of your favorite bourbon
Orange slice
Simple syrup (or one sugar cube and a splash of water) Orange bitters
Cherries

Preparation

1. Place simple syrup (or sugar cube) in an old fashioned glass with a few dashes of orange bitters.

2. Add a splash of water, a cocktail cherry and an orange slice.

3. Muddle ingredients well.

4. Fill your glass with ice cubes and add your bourbon.

5. Stir well.

6. Garnish with an orange slice or zest, and a cherry.

Tony says: This is the standard. The classic. Old Reliable. This is the drink of men and women and refined palates across the globe. Bitters and simple syrup are ingredients you should have on hand. They are easy to obtain, or, in the case of simple syrup, easy to make.

When I make simple syrup in a bigger batch than a sugar cube, I use the very easy to remember, "1 to 1 equals syrup." Start with 1 cup of boiling water, stir in 1 cup of sugar, and stir constantly until dissolved. Let it cool slightly, pour it into a container with a lid, and store it in the refrigerator. It's that easy.

* * *

Manhattan

Ingredients

2-2.5 oz. of your favorite bourbon
1 oz. of sweet vermouth
Cocktail cherries
2 dashes of Angostura bitters (optional)

Preparation

1. Pour your bourbon, sweet vermouth, and bitters into an ice-filled mixing glass.

2. Stir until chilled, and strain into glass.

3. Garnish with a couple of cocktail cherries.

4. Add a splash of cherry juice.

Tony says: The Old Fashioned and Manhattan are very, very close cousins. It's really just a taste question of how sweet you want to go that night ... or afternoon ... or morning. We don't judge. As for the "optional" on the bitters, that may be heresy to some. But again, we don't judge. If you're asking me, bitters are an essential part of the drink. Use them.

* * *

Whiskey Sour

Ingredients

2 oz. of your favorite bourbon .75 oz. of lemon
juice
.75 oz. of simple syrup Orange slice
Maraschino cherry

Preparation

1. Combine bourbon, lemon juice and simple
syrup in to an ice-filled shaker.

2. Shakewell.

3. Pour into a rocks glass over ice.

4. Add the orange slice and cherry for garnish.

Fingers says: This is a very simple recipe. Some
will add a little egg white to give their whiskey
sour a creamy texture, but it isn't necessary. If
you don't have simple syrup, check out Tony's
comments under the Old Fashioned recipe.

* * *

Boulevardier

Ingredients

1.5 oz. of your favorite bourbon 1 oz. Campari
1 oz. sweet vermouth
Orange twist

Preparation *(While this drink is popular served up, we think it's best on the rocks. Try them both with friends, and decide for yourself.)*

1. Put some ice in a cocktail glass.

2. Add your Campari, sweet vermouth and bourbon.

3. Stir well.

4. Add an orange twist.

Fingers says: There are people who like to use rye instead of bourbon in their Boulevardier, but for me, bourbon is the choice! The addition of Campari to this cocktail makes it less sweet than a Manhattan.

* * *

Kentucky Mule

Ingredients

2 oz. of your favorite bourbon .5 oz. of lime
juice
Ginger beer
Mint garnish (optional)

Preparation *(This drink is properly served in a copper
mug. But if you don't have one, it's not a problem. Use a
glass, and put copper mugs on your holiday wish list.)*

1. Pour your bourbon and lime juice into
   your mug or glass.

2. Add ice.

3. Top off your mug or glass with ginger
   beer.

Fingers says: Many will say you shouldn't make
a mule without a copper mug, but not everyone
has copper mugs lying around the house. There's
nothing wrong with enjoying your Kentucky
Mule from a glass. Don't let perfect be the enemy
of the good!

* * *

Bonus Recipes!

First, a twist on a traditional Sazerac...

Sazerac

Ingredients

2 oz. of your favorite bourbon
5 dashes of Peychaud's bitters
Simple syrup or a muddled sugar cube Absinthe
Lemon peel

Preparation

1. Set aside a chilled cocktail glass.

2. Splash the bitters into a mixing glass.

3. Add your bourbon into the mixing glass.

4. Add ice and stir well.

5. Add a touch of Absinthe to the bottom of your chilled glass. Coat the entire inside of the cocktail glass with your Absinthe by tilting the glass on its side and spinning.

6. Discard any extra Absinthe from your glass.

7. Using a strainer, pour your bitters and bourbon into your chilled glass.

8. Garnish with a lemon peel.

Tony says: Before going further, you should know the story of the Sazerac.

I had not heard of the drink before. So, when it was first brought up to me, I thought it was a reference to Sazerac Rye from Buffalo Trace. (Which, full disclosure, I think is wonderful.)

The Sazerac has a great history. Not only is it the official drink of New Orleans (which is really saying something, considering the popularity of the Hurricane during Mardi Gras), it also dates back to the 1800s. Originally, it was made with French brandy. And Peychaud's bitters was named after the New Orleans resident who created it. Rye replaced the brandy in the 1900s because it was far more plentiful and probably a great deal cheaper.

Two important things to remember with this drink. First, you have to dump the Absinthe before making the drink. It is there to add residual flavor, thus the coating of the glass. If you leave it in the final product, what you have is not a Sazerac. And, in my view, not very good.

Second, our recipe eliminates the rye and cognac completely, replacing it with bourbon. This is either right or wrong, depend- ing on who you are. We did it this way because this book focuses on bourbon. If you want to make a Sazerac in the "proper" way, replace the bourbon with 1.25 oz. of your favorite rye and 1.25 oz. of cognac.

Can you still use cognac (1.25 oz.) even if you use bourbon? Yes! Of course! Just bring the bourbon down to 1.25 oz. as well. Try it in every variation and see what works best for you.

* * *

Hot Toddy

Ingredients

2 oz. of your favorite bourbon
Hot water
Honey
1 tsp. of lemon juice
Lemon slice for garnish
Cinnamon stick (or a pinch of cinnamon)
Preparation

1. Pour 6oz. of hot water into your glass or mug

2. Add 2 tbsp. of honey and your lemon juice

3. Stir well.

4. Add your favorite bourbon and the lemon slice.

5. Stir again.

6. Add the cinnamon stick on top.

Fingers says: Whether you are coming down with a cold or coming in from it, a hot toddy is good for the soul. Seriously, it's medicinal! Some people like to use tea in their recipe, but for me it's not necessary. The bourbon, honey, and cinnamon are the stars of the show.

* * *

GREAT NAMES IN BOURBON HISTORY

These are some of the forefathers, the visionaries, and current great names in the history of bourbon. Sing their praises!

***

Carl Beam was a master distiller and vice president of the James B. Beam Distillery. Kentucky Bourbon Hall of Fame inductee, 2006.

Charlie Beam was a master distiller for Four Roses Distillery. Under his leadership, Four Roses released Benchmark Bourbon and Eagle Rare. Kentucky Bourbon Hall of Fame inductee, 2010.

David M. Beam was the founder of D. M. Beam & Company. He made Old Tub Bourbon a national brand. Kentucky Bourbon Hall of Fame inductee, 2009.

Earl Beam was a master distiller at Jim Beam Distillery, and later, Heaven Hill Distillery. He introduced HH's flagship brand, Evan Williams, in 1957. Kentucky Bourbon Hall of Fame inductee, 2003.

Edward Baker Beam was a head distiller at Jim Beam Distillery. He helped develop Jim Beam Black Double Aged Bourbon. Kentucky Bourbon Hall of Fame inductee, 2007.

Jacob Beam was a farmer who used his excess corn and his father's whiskey recipe to create his Old Jake Beam Sour Mash in 1795. His bourbon launched the Beam family into the whiskey business.

Colonel James B. Beam assumed leadership of the Old Tub Distillery before Prohibition. After Prohibition, he founded the Jim B. Beam Distilling Company. Kentucky Bourbon Hall of Fame inductee, 2002.

John Henry "Jack" Beam was a distiller and is best known as the inventor of Early Times. Kentucky Bourbon Hall of Fame inductee, 2009.

Parker Beam was a grandnephew of Jim Beam, and is best known for his work as a master distiller at Heaven Hill Distilleries. While there, he created Heaven Hill's first small batch bourbon, the Elijah Craig Small Batch. Kentucky Bourbon Hall of Fame inductee, 2001.

T. Jeremiah Beam took over the James B. Beam Distilling Co. in 1946. Under his leadership, Jim Beam became a global force. Kentucky Bourbon Hall of Fame inductee, 2005.

Isaac Wolfe Bernheim is remembered for being the founder of Bernheim Distillery, then maker of I.W. Harper Kentucky Straight Bourbon Whiskey. Kentucky Bourbon Hall of Fame inductee, 2012.

Colonel Albert Bacon Blanton was the president of the George T. Stagg Distillery. Under his leadership, the distillery survived Prohibition by applying for, and being awarded, one of only six special government licenses to produce "medicinal whiskey." Kentucky Bourbon Hall of Fame inductee, 2005.

George Garvin Brown was a pharmaceutical salesman turned distiller. He opened what would later become the Brown-Forman Distillery. Kentucky Bourbon Hall of Fame inductee, 2002.

Owsley Brown was the son of George Garvin Brown and former president of the Brown-Forman Corporation. Under his leadership, the distillery survived Prohibition by applying for, and being awarded, one of only six special government licenses to produce "medicinal whiskey." Kentucky Bourbon Hall of Fame inductee, 2008.

Owsley Brown II was the great-grandson of Brown-Forman's founder, George Garvin Brown. He was the chairman and CEO of Brown-Forman and expanded it internationally. Kentucky Bourbon Hall of Fame inductee, 2015.

Augustus Bulleit was an 1830s tavern keeper in Louisville. He created a unique bourbon that inspired the modern Bulleit Bourbon. Bulleit mysteriously vanished while transporting his juice from Kentucky to New Orleans. He was never seen again.

Thomas E. Bulleit, Jr. founded the Bulleit Distilling Company in 1987, reviving his old family recipe for a new generation of bourbon enthusiasts. Kentucky Bourbon Hall of Fame inductee, 2009.

Sam K. Cecil was a vice president of production for the Maker's Mark Distillery. Kentucky Bourbon Hall of Fame inductee, 2003.

Elijah Craig was a Baptist preacher turned distiller. He opened his distillery around 1789. Craig became the first distiller to age his whiskey in new charred oak barrels. Heaven Hill Distillery calls him "The Father of Bourbon" and named a brand of bourbon in his honor.

Dr. James Crow was a chemist/doctor who is credited with inventing the sour mash method of distilling whiskey. His Old Crow bourbon was once one of the most popular bourbons in America.

Ronnie Eddins was a barrel management expert for the Buffalo Trace Distillery. Eddins was one of the main forces behind the Buffalo Trace Bourbon Experimental Whiskey Program. Kentucky Bourbon Hall of Fame inductee, 2010.

Edwin S. Foote was a master distiller at the Old Fitzgerald Distillery. Kentucky Bourbon Hall of Fame inductee, 2008.

George Forman was George Garvin Brown's onetime accountant, who turned business partner. The Brown-Forman Distillery was formed in 1890.

William F. Friel was a master distiller and manager of Barton Brands. Kentucky Bourbon Hall of Fame inductee, 2006.

Gary R. Gayheart was a master distiller at the Buffalo Trace Distillery. He helped develop Blanton's, which was the world's first commercially sold single barrel bourbon. Kentucky Bourbon Hall of Fame inductee, 2007.

Oscar Getz was the founder of the Barton Distillery, later named Barton Brands. Getz was an author, historian, and lecturer who was inducted into the Kentucky Bourbon Hall of Fame in 2002.

Basil Hayden Sr. led a settlement of over 100 Catholics from 25 families to settle on land in Bardstown, Kentucky in 1785. This area of the Bluegrass State later became home to many famous bourbon brands, and is now known as the "Bourbon Capital of the World."

Lincoln Wesley Henderson was director of whiskey development and maturation, and a master distiller for Brown-Forman Beverages Worldwide. Lincoln was instrumental in creating Woodford Reserve, and later, Angel's Envy. Kentucky Bourbon Hall of Fame inductee, 2001.

Wes Henderson is the co-founder and chief innovation officer of the Louisville Distilling Company. He has continued to honor Lincoln Wesley Henderson's legacy with Angel's Envy. Kentucky Bourbon Hall of Fame inductee, 2019.

Freddie Johnson is the distillery VIP visitor lead (and storyteller extraordinaire) for the Buffalo Trace Distillery. Kentucky Bourbon Hall of Fame inductee, 2018.

Paul Jones, Jr. was the founder of Paul Jones & Company and trademarked Four Roses Bourbon in the 1860s. Kentucky Bourbon Hall of Fame inductee, 2003.

Even Kulsveen is the executive director of Willett Distillery. Kulsveen, along with his wife, Martha, oversaw the growth of Willett's brands. At a time when the popularity in bourbon declined in the U.S., he helped Willett grow in the Asian market. Kentucky Bourbon Hall of Fame inductee, 2019.

Elmer T. Lee was a WWII veteran who joined what would later be called the Buffalo Trace Distillery as a maintenance engineer in 1949. He eventually served as plant manager and master distiller until his retirement in 1985. In retirement, Lee served as master distiller emeritus and ambassador for Buffalo Trace Distillery. Kentucky Bourbon Hall of Fame inductee, 2001.

Thomas R. McCarthy was the founder of the J.T.S. Brown Distillery — later named the Wild Turkey Distillery. Kentucky Bourbon Hall of Fame inductee, 2004.

Thomas S. Moore was the founder of Tom Moore Distillery, which is now the site of the Barton 1792 Distillery. Kentucky Bourbon Hall of Fame inductee, 2007.

Chris Morris is a master distiller for Brown-Forman Corporation. If you love Woodford Reserve, you have Chris to thank. Kentucky Bourbon Hall of Fame inductee, 2017.

Steve Nally was the master distiller at Maker's Mark Distillery for over 30 years. He's currently a master distiller at the Bardstown Bourbon Company. Kentucky Bourbon Hall of Fame inductee, 2007.

Austin Nichols was a wholesale grocer who sold wine and bourbon back in the 1850s. The business he started would later own Wild Turkey.

Frederick Booker Noe II was a master distiller emeritus at Jim Beam Brands. He was the sixth generation of his family to head the distillery that was founded in 1795. Kentucky Bourbon Hall of Fame inductee, 2001.

Frederick Booker Noe III is a master distiller of the Jim Beam Brands Company. Noe is the great-grandson of Jim Beam, a seventh generation distiller, and a Kentucky Bourbon Hall of Fame inductee (in 2013).

Ernest W. Ripy Jr. was a former master distiller of Ripy Brothers Distillery. Ripy spent 42 years in the bourbon industry. Kentucky Bourbon Hall of Fame inductee, 2003.

Eddie Russell is a master distiller at the Wild Turkey Distillery. He is the co-creator of Russell's Reserve, Wild Turkey Kentucky Straight Bourbon Whiskey, and Rye and Rare Breed Rye. Kentucky Bourbon Hall of Fame inductee, 2010.

Jimmy Russell is a master distiller at the Wild Turkey Distillery. A 60-year whiskey veteran, Russell is the longest-tenured, active master distiller in the global spirits industry. Kentucky Bourbon Hall of Fame inductee, 2016.

Jim Rutledge is a former master distiller of Four Roses Distilling Company. He currently owns J.W. Rutledge Distillery. Credited as the man who saved Four Roses, Rutledge was inducted into the Kentucky Bourbon Hall of Fame in 2001.

Bill Samuels Jr. was the president and chairman emeritus of Maker's Mark. He is the son of Maker's Mark founders, Bill and Margie Samuels. He introduced Maker's 46 to market in 2010 — the first new brand for Maker's Mark in over 50 years. Kentucky Bourbon Hall of Fame inductee, 2001.

Bill Samuels Sr. was the co-founder of Maker's Mark Distillery. Samuels was a sixth generation distiller, and was inducted into the Kentucky Bourbon Hall of Fame in 2002.

Margie Samuels was the co-founder of Maker's Mark Distillery. The brand's signature red wax on every bottle was her creation. Kentucky Bourbon Hall of Fame inductee, 2014.

C. Orville Schupp was the president of Schenley Distillers, Inc. Before that, Schupp was a master distiller at the George T. Stagg Distillery. Kentucky Bourbon Hall of Fame inductee, 2003.

David, Ed, Gary, George, and Mose Shapira were the founders of Heaven Hill Distilleries. Shortly after it was founded, the Shapiras released Old Heaven Hill Bottled-in-Bond. Shortly after, it became the best-selling whiskey in the state of

Kentucky. Kentucky Bourbon Hall of Fame inductees, 2002.

Harry J. Shapira was an executive vice president of Heaven Hill Brands, Inc. Along with Max Shapira, he was part of the second generation of leadership that ran Heaven Hill Distillery. The Bourbon Heritage Center and the Evan Williams Bourbon Experience were his pet projects. Kentucky Bourbon Hall of Fame inductee, 2017.

Max L. Shapira is the president of Heaven Hill Brands, Inc. Along with Harry Shapira, he was part of the second generation of leadership that ran Heaven Hill Distillery. He is a Kentucky Bourbon Hall of Fame inductee (2018) and a recipient of the Parker Beam Lifetime Achievement Award.

Matthew J. Shattock was the chairman & CEO of Beam Suntory, where he oversaw its growth from 2009-2020. Bourbon Hall of Fame inductee, 2018.

George T. Stagg is considered one of the founding fathers of the modern day Buffalo Trace Distillery. Kentucky Bourbon Hall of Fame inductee, 2002.

Peggy Noe Stevens is the founder and president of Peggy Noe Stevens & Associates. Peggy was the world's first female master bourbon taster. Kentucky Bourbon Hall of Fame inductee, 2019.

President William Howard Taft was the 27th president of the United States. Taft crafted *The Taft Decision*, which answered the question, "What is Whisky?" Kentucky Bourbon Hall of Fame inductee, 2009.

Colonel Frank B. Thompson was the chairman of Glenmore Distilleries. His leadership helped guide Glenmore through Prohibition. Kentucky Bourbon Hall of Fame inductee, 2002.

W. L. Weller was the founder of W. L. Weller & Sons, a liquor wholesale business. He was also a master distiller who was the first to use wheat instead of rye in his mash bill. William Larue Weller started selling his wheated bourbon in 1848.

Evan Williams founded Kentucky's first commercial distillery on the banks of the Ohio River in 1783. Kentucky Bourbon Hall of Fame inductee, 2008.

Julian P. "Pappy" Van Winkle Sr. was a liquor salesman turned distiller. He was the founder of the Stitzel-Weller Distillery. Some of the world's most expensive bourbon is named after him. Kentucky Bourbon Hall of Fame inductee, 2002.

* * *

7

QUOTES

We set out to find the most meaningful quotes and phrases ever uttered about bourbon and whiskey in general. Consider them your daily devotional. Or, your daily inspiration. Or, something you read while you go to the bathroom.

* * *

"That's the problem with drinking, I thought, as I poured myself a drink. If something bad happens you drink in an attempt to forget; if something good happens you drink in order to celebrate; and if nothing happens you drink to make something happen."

— Charles Bukowski (1920-1994) *German-American poet, novelist, and short story writer. In 1986 Time Magazine called Bukowski a "laureate of American lowlife".*

Fingers says: That's the good thing about drinking, as I write this with a drink next to me. If something bad happens a drink will help you forget; if something good happens, you should continue to drink because more good things will happen; and something *will* happen, so keep drinking.

Unless the drink is Fireball.

* * *

"I feel bad for people who don't drink. When they wake up in the morning, that's as good as they're going to feel all day."

— Frank Sinatra (1915-1998) *American singer and actor. One of the greatest musical artists of the 20th century.*

Fingers says: Frank's go-to drink was Jack Daniels, on the rocks, with a little water. He loved it so much that when he died at the age of 82, he was buried with a bottle of Old No. 7.

Tony says: My wife loves Jack Daniels. And that's why she's my wife.

* * *

"Drink because you are happy, but never because you are miserable."

— G.K. Chesterton (1874-1936) *English writer, philosopher, lay theologian, and literary and art critic.*

Tony says: I agree with this, wholeheartedly. Misery drinking will never work out. It's like a business idea at midnight. It sounds good at the time, but in the light of day it'll bankrupt you.

* * *

"I don't have a drinking problem. 'Cept when I can't get a drink."

— Tom Waits (1949-Present). *American singer, musician, songwriter, composer, and actor. In 2015 Rolling Stone Magazine ranked Waits No. 55 on "100 Greatest Songwriters of All Time".*

Fingers says: I kick myself when I look in my liquor cabinet and realize that the bottle I thought I had in there is gone.

Tony says: If there is still something in the liquor cabinet, you're doing all right.

* * *

"To alcohol! The cause of … and solution to … all of life's problems."

— Homer Simpson *Nuclear safety inspector, Springfield Nuclear Power Plant.*

Fingers says: Alcohol may have gotten me into trouble a couple of times. Like that night I spent in a Cancún jail cell, or the time I found out I bought all that Enron stock two years after it went bankrupt.

I certainly couldn't drink my way out of those problems.

But man, have I tried…

Tony says: Is there anything Homer has ever gotten wrong? Ever? He is the perfect specimen of manhood, and his advice should be heeded. Always.

* * *

"Alcohol, taken in sufficient quantities, may produce all the effects of drunkenness."

— Oscar Wilde (1854-1900). *Irish poet and playwright.*

Tony says: The same can be said of chocolate cake and fatness.

Fingers says: The same can be said for eating Tide Pods and stupidity.

Also, don't eat Tide Pods.

* * *

"They're professionals at this in Russia, so no matter how many Jell-O shots or Jager shooters you might have downed at college mixers, no matter how good a drinker you might think you are, don't forget that the Russians — any Russian — can drink you under the table."

— Anthony Bourdain (1956-2018) *American celebrity chef, author, and travel documentarian.*

Fingers says: Back when the Soviet Union fell, and Boris Yeltsin took over Russia, he looked like he could run a country on a fifth of vodka before noon! So, what hope would the average American have trying to out-drink Yeltsin? He could still probably drink all of us under the table, and he died in 2007.

* * *

"The light music of whiskey falling into a glass — an agreeable interlude."

— James Joyce (1882-1941) *Irish novelist, short story writer, poet, teacher, and literary critic. Regarded as one of the most influential and important writers of the 20th century.*

Tony says: This quote? This is why I will never write as well as James Joyce.

Fingers says: Bourbon is an escape, yet also an enhancer of good times with friends. And it's 100 times better than any song by Train.

* * *

"Nothing uses up alcohol faster than political argument."

— Robert A. Heinlein (1907-1988). *American science fiction author, aeronautical engineer, and naval officer.*

Tony says: Clearly, Heinlein was never a Lions fan.

Fingers says: Bourbon is a political observer's best friend. That, and a mute button.

* * *

"My own experience has been that the tools I need for my trade are paper, tobacco, food, and a little whisky."

— William Faulkner (1897-1962). *One of the most celebrated writers of American Literature.*

* * *

"A drink centers me but I usually make myself wait until at least 9 p.m. for that. Or 8 p.m. Whichever comes first."

— Bill Callahan (1966-Present) *American singer-songwriter.*

* * *

"Always carry a flagon of whiskey in case of snakebite and furthermore always carry a small snake."

— W.C. Fields (1880-1946) *American comedian, actor, and writer.*

Fingers says: Listen, I love flasks. And when you're out and about and people know you have pocket bourbon, well, you become the most popular guy they know.

Just make sure you clean that thing. A dirty flask is gross. So is a small snake.

* * *

"I drink to make other people more interesting."

— Ernest Hemingway (1899-1961) *American novelist, short-story writer, journalist, and sportsman. His novel, "The Old Man and the Sea," won the Pulitzer Prize and the Nobel Prize in Literature.*

Fingers says: Drinking makes social media more interesting. I like mixing bourbon with Twitter.

...I really should delete my Twitter account.

* * *

"I have taken more out of alcohol than alcohol has taken out of me."

— Winston Churchill (1874-1965). *Prime Minister of the United Kingdom from 1940 to 1945, during the Second World War, and again from 1951 to 1955.*

Tony says: Sir Winston Churchill did more to solidify the value of whiskey than Kim Kardashian did to solidify the value of sex tapes. Kim, however, made far more money.

* * *

"Scientists announced that they have located the gene for alcoholism. Scientists say they found it at a party, talking way too loudly."

— Conan O'Brien (1963-Present). *American television host, comedian, writer, podcaster, and producer.*

Fingers says: Give me the loud drinker over that other kind of person … the angry loner. The one who sits in the corner. Plotting … scheming … plotting.

He's the guy who usually led me into trouble.

* * *

"Ninety percent I'll spend on good times, women, and Irish whisky. The other ten percent I'll probably waste."

— Tug McGraw (1944-2004) *American Baseball player.*

* * *

"A man is a fool if he drinks before he reaches the age of 50, and a fool if he doesn't afterward."

— Frank Lloyd Wright (1867-1959) *American architect, designer, writer, and educator.*

Tony says: Dreadful advice. Let Frank design buildings.

* * *

"A bartender is just a pharmacist with a limited inventory."

— Albert Einstein (1879-1955) *German-born theoretical physicist. Best known for developing the theory of relativity.*

Fingers says: A bartender is a pharmacist, psychiatrist, couple's counselor, financial advisor, and den mother. As a former bartender, the best part about giving advice is knowing it will most likely be forgotten by morning.

* * *

"If I cannot drink bourbon and smoke cigars in Heaven then I shall not go."

— Mark Twain (1835-1910) *American writer, humorist, entrepreneur, publisher, and lecturer. He is known as the greatest humorist the United States has ever produced.*

Tony says: There is nothing in the world that Mark Twain has not put his spin on. And even fewer things where his spin is incorrect.

* * *

"If you drink, don't drive. Don't even putt."

— Dean Martin (1917-1995) *American singer, actor and comedian.*

Fingers says: Got to disagree with Deano on this one. I love having a drink on the golf course. It helps me putt. Just don't get drunk on the course. It can lead to bad things.

Bad, bad things.

* * *

"Whisky is liquid sunshine."

— George Bernard Shaw (1856-1950) *Irish playwright, critic, polemicist and political activist. 1925 winner of the Nobel Prize for Literature.*

Fingers says: Nations may fall. Fads come and go. But bourbon is forever. Just like Betty White.

* * *

"I should never have switched from Scotch to Martinis."

— Humphrey Bogart (1899-1957) *American film and stage actor.*

Fingers says: For me, drinking a martini is like drinking gasoline. It reminds me of a quote from the great Frank Drebin — "It's like eating a spoonful of Drano. Sure it will clean you out, but it'll leave you hollow inside."

Tony says: Bogart (and Fingers) are wrong here. Martinis, made right, are quite fine. Bogart also got Lauren Bacall. For that alone, he's entitled to make a mistake here or there.

* * *

"You can handle just about anything that comes at you out on the road with a believable grin, common sense, and whiskey."

— Bill Murray (1950-Present) *American actor, comedian, and writer.*

* * *

"There is no bad whiskey. There are only some whiskeys that aren't as good as others."

— Raymond Chandler (1888-1959) *American-British novelist and screenwriter.*

Fingers says: That's one reason why we have cocktails. Find a bourbon that's not your favorite on the rocks? Use it to make an Old Fashioned. Try it in a Kentucky Mule.

Point is, you can salvage the whiskey that doesn't do it for you. Check out the recipes in this book!

* * *

"Happiness is having a rare steak, a bottle of whiskey, and a dog to eat the rare steak."

— Johnny Carson (1925-2005) *American television host, comedian, writer, and producer. Host of 'The Tonight Show Starring Johnny Carson' from 1962-1992.*

Fingers says: Johnny should have tried the reverse-sear method for his rare steak! Throw that steak on the grill on very low heat, around 225 degrees. Let it cook low and slow until the internal temperature of the steak gets to about 110 degrees.

Pull that meat off your grill, and fire it up to 500 degrees. Put the steak back on (at two minutes a side) to get a nice sear. It's a perfect steak to go along with that whiskey.

* * *

"I wish to live to 150 years old, but the day I die, I wish it to be with a cigarette in one hand and a glass of whiskey in the other."

— Ava Gardner (1922-1990) *American actress and singer.*

Tony says: A fair amount of men would rather that, on their 150th birthday, they had a glass of whiskey in one hand and Ava Gardner in the other.

* * *

"I have never in my life seen a Kentuckian who didn't have a gun, a pack of cards, and a jug of whiskey."

— President Andrew Jackson (1767-1845) *American lawyer, soldier, and statesman. Served as the seventh President of the United States from 1829 to 1837.*

Fingers says: If true, then let me say proudly that Today, We Are All Kentuckians!

* * *

"Bourbon does for me what the piece of cake did for Proust."

— Walker Percy (1916-1990) *American writer of philosophical novels and essays in the Southern Gothic literary movement. Published "Bourbon" in 1975, an essay on the aesthetic of Bourbon drinking.*

* * *

"It is true that whisky improves with age. The older I get, the more I like it."

— Ronnie Corbett (1930-2016) *Scottish actor, broadcaster, comedian and writer.*

* * *

"God invented whiskey to keep the Irish from ruling the world."

— Ed McMahon (1923-2009) *American announcer, game show host, comedian, actor, singer and combat aviator. Sideman and announcer for Johnny Carson on NBC's The Tonight Show Starring Johnny Carson from 1962 to 1992.*

Tony says: This quote, said in today's world, would get Ed destroyed on social media. Then again, if Ed were alive today, there is no way he'd be on social media.

Fingers says: This is ridiculous. I'm Irish and I don't touch the stuff.

Tony says: He touches the stuff.

Fingers says: Yeah. I do.

* * *

"A good gulp of hot whiskey at bedtime — it's not very scientific, but it helps."

— Alexander Fleming (1881-1955) *Scottish physician and microbiologist who discovered penicillin.*

Fingers says: I love science! And while I don't like hot whiskey, it's hard to argue that a strong hot toddy wouldn't make someone feel a little better, sick or not.

* * *

"Giving money and power to government is like giving whiskey and car keys to teenage boys."

— P. J. O'Rourke (1947-Present) *American political satirist and journalist.*

Tony says: Never give whiskey to a teenager. Never give power to government. Those are good rules to live by.

* * *

"Bourbon is a comfort food. As the world becomes more complex, bourbon remains simple."

— Reid Mitenbuler (1978-Present) *Author of "Bourbon Empire: The Past and Future of America's Whiskey"*

* * *

"There's nothing mysterious about the art of tasting bourbon. Some bourbons are best enjoyed neat, others with a splash of water; still others lend themselves to mixing cocktails."

— Susan Reigler (1955-Present) *Certified Executive Bourbon Steward, author of "Kentucky Bourbon Country: The Essential Travel Guide"*

Fingers says: People ask me all the time, "What's the best way to enjoy a bourbon? Neat? On the rocks?"

We say it all the time on the show — the best way to drink bourbon is how YOU like to drink bourbon. Don't let anyone shame you into drinking it a certain way. Bourbon is made to be enjoyed, and only you know how you enjoy your bourbon. Cheers!

* * *

8

FIND US

Eat! Drink! Smoke! is everywhere. And our relationship doesn't end with the end of this book. Listen on the radio, listen to the podcast, visit the website, check out the reviews and interactions on social media.

And let us know what you thought of the book!

Website: eatdrinksmokeshow.com

Instagram: @eatdrinksmokepodcast

Facebook: facebook.com/eatdrinksmoke

Twitter: @goeatdrinksmoke

Find Your Local Station: eatdrinksmokeshow.com/stations

ABOUT THE AUTHORS

Tony Katz (left) and Fingers Malloy are the hosts
of the nationally syndicated **Eat! Drink! Smoke!**
radio program.

This is their first book.
This is not their first bourbon.

INDEX

We sourced everything as well as we could. If you spot an omission, or have a comment. Email LetsGoBourbon@eatdrinksmokeshow.com.

1 - https://collections.library.appstate.edu/research-aids/bourbon-americas-native-spirit

2 - https://www.distillerytrail.com/blog/when-did-bourbon-whiskey-become-a-distinctive-product-of-the-united-states/

3 - https://www.law.cornell.edu/cfr/text/27/5.22

4- https://www.jackdaniels.com/en-us/faqs

5 - https://www.distillerytrail.com/blog/bottled-in-bond-act-signed-into-law-march-3-1897-the-law-explained-by-fred-bernie-video/

6 - https://www.americanbourbonassociation.com/what-bourbon

These resources were also used:

KYBourbon.com, Whiskeyuniv.com, JimBeam.com, FourRosesBourbon.com, HeavenHillDistillery.com, Brown-Forman.com, Bulleit.com, MakersMark.com, ElijahCraig.com, BuffaloTraceDistillery.com, KentuckyBourbonWhiskey.com and WildTurkeyBourbon.com